Librarians

Laura K. Murray

CREATIVE EDUCATION • CREATIVE PAPERBACKS

seedlings

Published by Creative Education and Creative Paperbacks
P.O. Box 227, Mankato, Minnesota 56002
Creative Education and Creative Paperbacks
are imprints of The Creative Company
www.thecreativecompany.us

Design by Ellen Huber
Production by Grant Gould
Art direction by Rita Marshall
Printed in the United States of America

Photographs by Alamy (Bob Daemmrich, Guerilla,
imageBROKER, Montgomery Martin, Steve Skjold,
Wavebreak Media ltd), Getty (Andersen Ross Photography,
Hill Street Studios, Maskot, Wavebreakmedia Ltd),
iStockphoto (clu, diignat, FatCamera, harmpeti, MeryVu,
urfinguss, Wavebreakmedia Ltd), Shutterstock (Atovot,
donatas1205, SofikoS)

ISBN 9781640264120 (library binding)
ISBN 9781628329452 (paperback)
ISBN 9781640005761 (eBook)

LCCN 2020907011

TABLE OF CONTENTS

Hello, librarians!

Librarians work in a library.

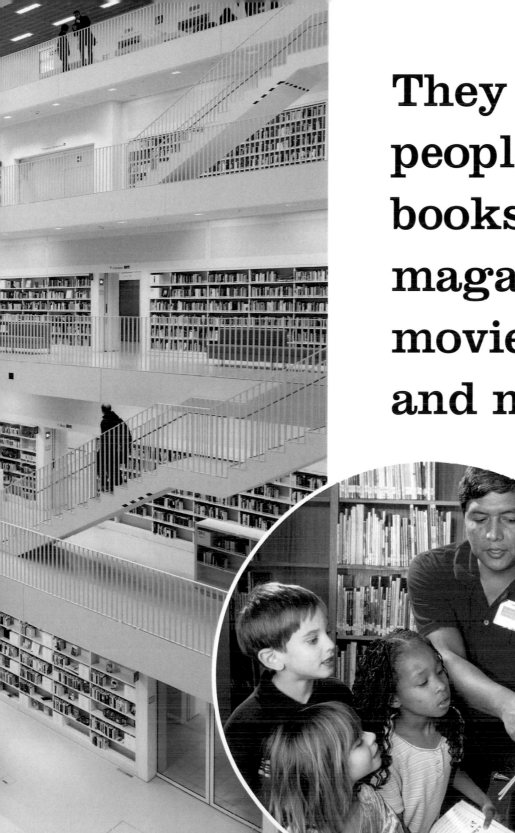

They help people find books, magazines, movies, music, and more.

Some librarians work in school libraries.

Others work in city libraries.

Anyone can go there.

Librarians may work on a bookmobile. It is a library on wheels! It travels from place to place.

People use library cards to check out books and other materials.

Then they bring them back. Librarians keep track of it all.

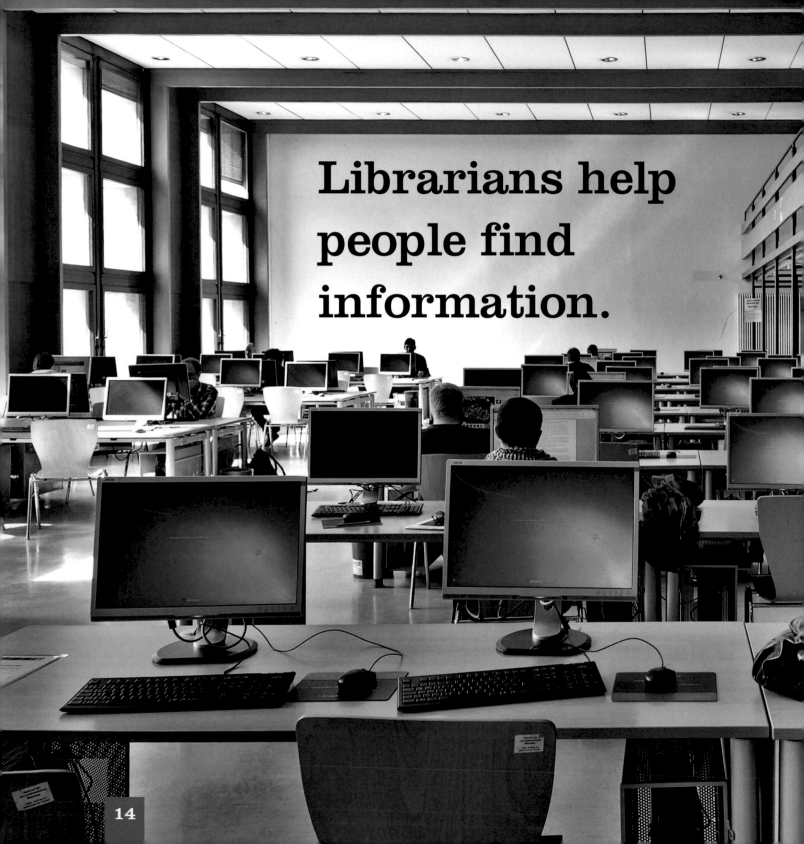

Librarians help people find information.

They help with computers and research. They find books and audiobooks.

Librarians read books
to children. They tell
stories. They lead
fun programs.

Thank you, librarians!

Picture a Librarian

shelves

books

cart

computer

scanner

desk

Words to Know

audiobooks: recordings of books being read out loud

check out: to borrow

programs: events or performances

research: to collect information

Read More

Moening, Kate. *Librarians.*
Minneapolis: Bellwether Media, 2019.

Roza, Greg. *My First Trip to the Library.*
New York: PowerKids Press, 2020.

Websites

Librarian Coloring Page
https://www.crayola.com/free-coloring-pages/print
/librarian-coloring-page/

Take a Field Trip to the Library
https://www.pbs.org/video/kidvision-vpk-shhhhh-were-
visiting-library

Index